No. 01　FOUND INSPIRATION MOVING FORWARD

WHiTE **FLUFFY** CLOUdS

No. AR　ENDOPHASIA PUBLICATIONS

french essentials

"How are you?" - "como talle vu?"

"Thank you for coming." - "Merci detra-vanu"

"who wants to sleep with the soundman?"
— Ki-vu dolmeer avec lu soundman

~~"ooh pu-regg tru-ve cola amborger vegetarian?"~~

ooh pu-regg tru-ve ah amborger vegetarian?

"Where could I find a vegetarian hamburger"

"Un za D.J. hat ein shvanz vee ein pfert!"
— our D.J. is hung like a horse!"

German

FIND

FOUND INSPIRATION MOVING FORWARD

WHiTE **FLUFFY** CLOUdS

Volume 01
10   03

WHITE FLUFFY CLOUDS
FOUND INSPIRATION MOVING FORWARD BY BRANDON BOYD

BRANDON BOYD
PAINTINGS : PHOTOGRAPHY : WRITINGS : THOUGHTS

MARK MURPHY
MURPHY : DESIGN : LAYOUT : WWW.MURPHYDESIGN.COM

ENDOPHASIA PUBLICATIONS
PUBLISHING COMPANY

HARD BOUND EDITION $35.00
ISBN0-9745120-0-1

COPYRIGHT © 2003 BRANDON BOYD AND ENSOPHASIA PUBLICATIONS
ALL ART WORKS COPYRIGHT ©2003 BRANDON BOYD
PRINTED IN CHINA

NO PART OF THIS BOOK MAY BE REPRODUCED OR TRANSMITTED IN ANY WAY
SHAPE OR FORM. ELECTRONIC OR MECHANICAL, INCLUDING PHOTOCOPY,
RECORDING OR ANY OTHER INFORMATION STORAGE AND RETRIEVAL SYSTEMS,
WITHOUT WRITTEN PERMISSION FROM THE PUBLISHER AND THE ARTIST.

Volume 01
10   03

SOFT DISCLAIM   E R

For those who partake in the findings of this book please excuse any and all grammatical errors you may come across. Upon closer scrutiny of this work, I felt that inconsistencies like those reflected the human aspects of this project (among other things). Or, maybe I was just too lazy to correct my mistakes. Anyway, I felt that spell checking it after the fact would make a geyser feel more like a sputter. Know-what-I'm-sayin?

Special thanks to my wonderful and supportive family, Carolyn Murphy and lil' Miss Dylan Bleu, the members of my band, Mark Murphy, Steve Rennie, Alix Sloan, Brian and Shea Bowen-Smith, all the teachers who lent their experience to me and continue to, and anyone else, past present or future who helped facilitate another schmuck just trying to live out his dreams. Thank you. Brandon

photos courtesy of Chris McCann on pgs. 01, 04, 49 and back cover and Darren Boyd on pages 21 and 22. thanks.

So you want to write a book? What on earth would you write about? The state of the world? Your life? The lives around you? I am not sure to tell you the truth. With the million and one things one could potentially write about, one can't help but think quite hard on numerous topics and invariably get a little flustered with the sheer magnitude of topics that have already been covered. And now my typewriter is acting funny and space locating for me.

It is quite funny actually, when I go into any bookstore. I get the same feeling I get these days when I enter a record store. It's the 'Holy Shit I have no idea what I wanted to buy' syndrome that paralyzes people and makes them just want to turn back and jack off in front of the television. Oversaturation. Plentification on a mass scale that dizzies the customer and makes alternatives seem rewarding. Though too many books and too many cd's is better than not enough, it doesn't make it any easier for the would be writer or musician who is usually swallowed whole by the mammoth mouth of supply and demand.

So the trick must be to write a book that is so fucking amazing that everyone talks about it uncontrollably therefore having an overwhelming need to rush out to their local Barnes and Noble to sweep up the first copies of said piece of literature. So life altering that it makes the New York Times Best Seller List 10 weeks running and the author is on Oprah andMaury Povich and Larry King and 'Book Talk' with David Flemming and 'The View' with Barbara Walters. (Just to name a few)

Writing isn't just writing anymore. It's networking, mass communication, multi-media multi-tasking, techno basket weaving and artful prose all rolled into one. Where the author is the Hero and his life's story after and before the book are more alluring than the fictional character he pulled from his ass.

"Brandon is a 15 year writer with PHds in Psychology, parapsychology, sociology, phrenology, and leftist-hungarian ontology. He received his first Master's in Bolivia where hestudied under none other than Confuscious himself and later was awarded the Nobel Peace Prize for his contributions to primate psychology and it's relationship to quantum mechanics. He is 27 years old and lives in Malibu with his girlfriend."

Or there's the ever popular, "Brandon's band hada string of success in the later part of the 20th century and thought that he could use his popularity as a singer and his high school education to pawn himself off as a pseudo-intellectual and sell some books to a few of the kids who bought his cd's. Knowing him and knowing the hard work he put into learning to read, we thought this seemed a litle harmless so we shan't begrudge him an extra 2 minutes in the light."

How does one know if one sucks? I mean how do you ever know if you are any good at what you do? The only real gage of our abilities is the feedback we get from our peers, but they are subject to the same relativist principles as the rest of us. And masses of people paying compliment to your work, in whatever form it might take, could indeed be a further indication of your suck-dom! For is it not true that the masses are asses? Think of the most prosperous bands in the United States today; they are the worst shit I have ever had the displeasure of hearing. White people co-opting urban cultures slang, styles and manerisms and making a fucking fortune in doing so. It is kind of sickening.

Not to dissimilar from the whole Elvis phenomenom of the last era. A suburban white kid steals the underground black culture's songs and ideas and becomes known as 'The King'!

But even the ones not rapping and 'O.G-ing' out suck. The adult contemporary movement popularized by the hybrid pop/ country/ christian rock singers. As if one of those three in the phrase wasn't enough crap on it's own, we get singers and bands that categorize all three! Wheee!!

I have just come to realize that I am a complaining piece of shit. The only things I can think to write about are my numerous complaints and grievances that I am too humble and reserved to speak aloud. I guess I could. Just complain out loud like the rest of the world I mean. But that would make me feel like the rest of the world. Outward and out of line. I have always felt that an impartial confidante couldn't exist in a human being. One that didn't charge by the hour at least. So I have become the introvert who spills the milk to one and only one source. The page. The pen. The song. (Well, three.) And how vain of me to do so and let others read it. Better yet, pay to read it. I guess there's some thick irony involved in taking the stance as the quiet complainer. As I am seeing tonight, I mouth off as much as the next spoiled Californian. I just have a different and more fiendish way of routing those frustrations.

I guess if I were to start again and choose my angst's mode of transport, I wouldn't really do it any differently. Perhaps I would just try and tell myself that somewhere, someone is reading it or listening to it or seeing it and thoroughly enjoying themselves. Be it out of pure entertainment and comedy, or because of the simple fact that they understand where it is I am coming from.

i had that dream again

i'm exploring my (own) home : i happen across a door : that leads me to a room i've never seen

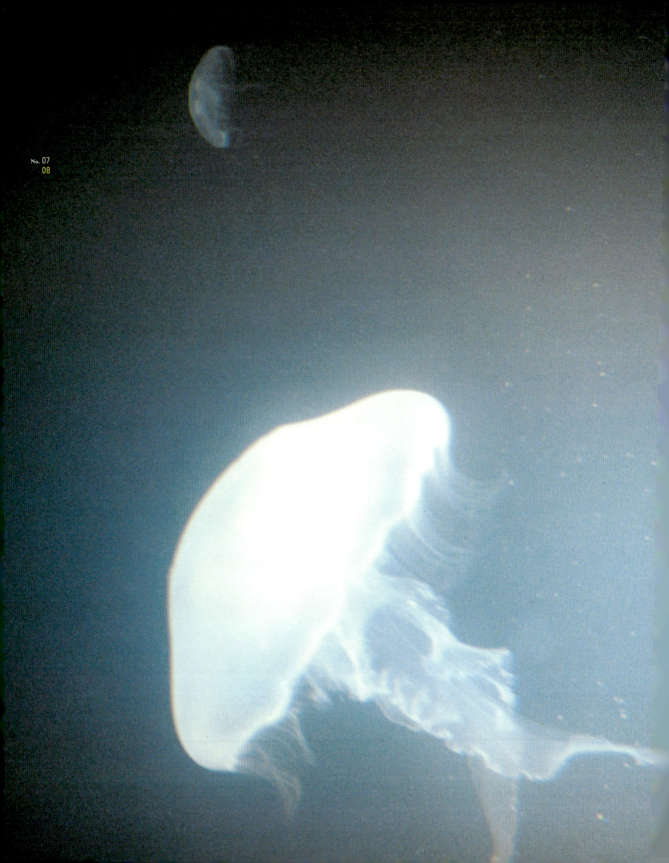

i think perhaps love thrives on unlikely circumstance and chance : life thrives on these principles,

and is life not love?

AND LOVE NOT LIFE?

HAIL, RIGHT BRAIN!

When you think of we;
  our society,
How much head-room
do you receive, and
therefore, acheive?
Don't be afraid to sum
it up poetically,
  illogically...
Hail the right brain.

(Jan. 1997)

No. 17
18

to think that one's actions could please the masses is indeed a notion bound in irony;

someone will inevitably find something wrong in almost everything.

so do what it is that you do best and remember to have enough tolerance for two.

(FEAR)

To say that I have an overactive imagination is indeed an understatement. Wether it was flying saucers, mischievious poltergiests pulling at my arm, my Mother's self portrait oil rendition of herself as the Virgin Mary, or the Big Bad Wolf coming up from the toilet bowl to eat my butt cheeks, I was constantly watching my back.

I wasn't paranoid, per say, But I definately had my finger on the pulse of the 'Twitchy Ten Year Old of the Nation Thing' going on. Whatever that means. Are all kids afraid of the dark? Did other adolescents growing up in our 'Healthy Fear of Russians' culture accept the true possibility that alien abduction was and still is a valid excuse for being late to school? Did the Big Bad Wolf fuck you all up as much as he did me? I'm sure we all had our things, as it were, but for some reason, he (the Big Bad Wolf) had me by the short and curlies! (Sparce as they were.)

I must have been five years old when it happened. Just minding my own business on the toilet; feet barely touching the ground, trying hard not to get my fingers stinky whilst whiping. You know, your average, run of the mill, "I gotta make B.M.'s" story. And then there he was. Strategically placed in amongst a less than suspicious looking children's book about three little fucking pigs. A story most likely created to harness the next generation's love of pork but instead created a kid who for the next five years would be afraid of anything resembling a German Shepard and who wouldn't take a shit on his own even if it meant having to change his underwear two to three times a day.

I became the family entertainment as I have been discovering over the past few years in that i would hold long and meaningful conversations with the bathroom door open with whomever was in closest proximity to my poop schedule. I even went as far as paying my younger, then impressionable, brother to accompany me to the bathroom. Knowing in my heart and with my instincts that that fucking wolf with his blood-drenched teeth, cold red eyes, and maniacal heart wouldn't dare trying anything with two of us in the bathroom! It went against the code of conduct for any terror wielding, fantasmagorical creature to do such things. Any and all victims had to be expressly alone and without bedsheets covering the head and or eyes.

Needless to say I survived those perilous loomings in the latrine; albeit a few dollars and change poorer. But now that I am old enough to recognize it, I am pissed off! I don't care who it is but I am gonna sue someone! Beit the publisher of the book, the illustrator of said piece, my Mom for painting herself as a religious icon, Steven Spielberg for imprinting extraterrestrial imagery onto my fragile, burgeoning subconscience, or myself for not having the where-with-all between the ages of five and ten to tell the difference. Get a lawyer dude, 'cause someone's gonna pay!

"I think perhaps love thrives on unlikely circumstance and chance. Life thrives on these principles, and is life not love? And love not life?"

(Sept. 1999)

'To think that one's actions could please the masses is indeed a notion bound in irony; someone will inevitably find something wrong in almost everything.
So do what it is that you do best, and remember to have enough tolerance for two.'

(Feb. 2000)

WHY IS IT EASIER TO PICK UP THE PEN WHEN I'M NOT HAPPY? WHY IS DILEMA THE AFRODISIAC OF THE WRITER. I WANT TO BE HAPPY, BUT I WANT TO WRITE. I AM FINDING THAT WHEN I'M CONTENT, I HAVE LESS TO WRITE ABOUT. WHY IS THIS.
PARADOX!
CAN THERE BE A MIDDLE GROUND? AND IF SO, WILL I FIND IT?

6/17/00

(You won't understand... you don't, could you please just try.)

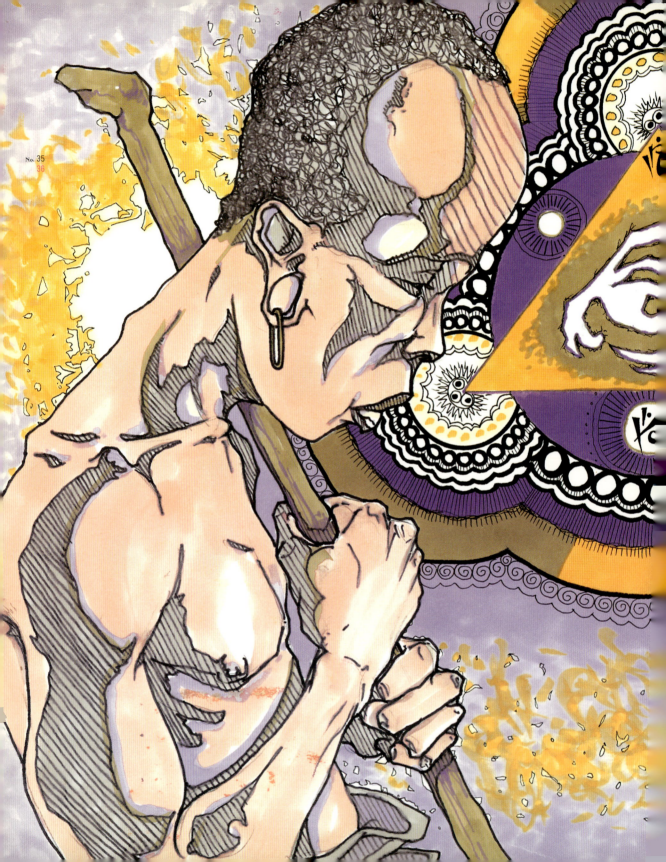

I STAY

I live under a tree.
I balance an apple on my head.
A man with a rusty revolver and
a twitching trigger finger
stands at spitting distance.
The man is high on gin, cigars and power.
There are many like me.
There are few like him.
 I was born with the apple on my head.
The gun was a gift to him.
He nods off occasionally;
stumbling, twitching and squeezing off
random bullets that graze all but
the apple in the process.
I've taken his bullets before;
hence fear & pain, but never
         finality.
I am not tied to this tree.
If I turn my head enough the apple falls.
My eventual assailant isn't the sharpest
tool in the shed.
I would barely be missed.
I could leave at any time.
     Yet, I stay.

Disconnect

Disconnect and let me drift until my upside-down is rightside in. Society must let the artist go to wander off into the nebula.

Upon return, I conjure what was seen—I let it pulse and boil within my limbs—I lay my pencil to the porous page and let my lunatic indulge itself.

No. 47
48

SOMEONE WILL INEVITABLY FIND SOMETHING WRONG IN ALMOST EVERYTHING.

so do what it is that you do best and remember to have enough tolerance for two.

inner voice
is yelling...

Watching the news is like cutting yourself with a dull blade over and over then pouring lemon juice into the wound. It completely eludes me as to why so many Americans can use it as their primary information source. And their daily variety entertainment to boot! I am not sure which one actually is more frightening; the pseudo-information source or the place of refuge!

We are a culture of self inflicted wounds. Defamation and spiritual mutilation. And how ironic that the practice of 'Body Manipulation' and or tattoo art and the like are so culturally frowned upon. These are people seen largely in everyday society as outcasts, heathens, self-destructive do-no-gooders, sinners, etc. But it conveniently escapes most people's observations that usually the people who choose life affirming practices like tattooing, ecstatic practice and artistic endeavors are more likely to not watch the news.

A vast majority of people watch the news. Whether it is for routine, sense of safety, entertainment or otherwise. And a vast majority of people in this country at least have an irrational fear of everything. Fear of their neighbors, fear of flying, fear of disease, fear of foreigners, fear of leaving the house. Or some might call them 'phobias'.

One might even deduce that we are a nurtured nation of... what's the fucking word I'm looking for? I don't know. A nation of 'Phobics' we'll say. We are taught to be afraid of everything. And it is so interesting that children, who come into the world so pure and true and full of hope and wonder are slowly taught to be this way. It's actually quite sick. You'd think that growing older would lend a sense of well being with the years it brought. You'd think that the more you knew the better of you'd be. It's funny because I can hear that stupid confuscian bit of nonsense in my head right now, "The more you learn, the less you know." Or something like that.

It infuriates me when I watch the news for more than five minutes! The way they start to tell you what the weather's gonna be like the next few days then stop and say, "After the break we'll really tell you the rest!" But then proceed to fill you up with as much ill-sigted negativity and bullshit so by the time they actually tell you what temperature it's going to be tomorrow you are to depressed to care and scared to leave the house!

"Terrorist threats are at an all-time high, and authorities are urging all southlanders to stalk up on duct tape, plastic sheeting and gas masks! But it'll be 76 degrees tomorrow and there's a parade at the Covina Muslim Community Center! Brent Goodman reprting."

Tomorrow I want to get a tattoo. I would like to plead with my parents to stop watching the news and come outside with me. Come out and play in the sun and leave their shoes and gasmasks at home. Leave the house unlocked and forget the turn on the answering machine. Forget to put sunblock spf 70 on our noses and get a little pink. Perhaps revel in eachother's presence and forget that the world is in a continuous state of emergency, the polar ice caps are melting, the government is irrevocably corrupt, missiles are in route to some innocent person's backyard and we probably sent them there, angry extremists are plotting their next dastardly debacle in a country we can barely pronounce, killer, africanized bees are in-route to our children's birthday parties, a high speed police pursuit is in progress as we speak, another faceless, corporate enterprise swindled billions from the poor, six tons of cocaine just made it across the Mexican border and is minutes away from hitting the streets, oh, and have a nice day.

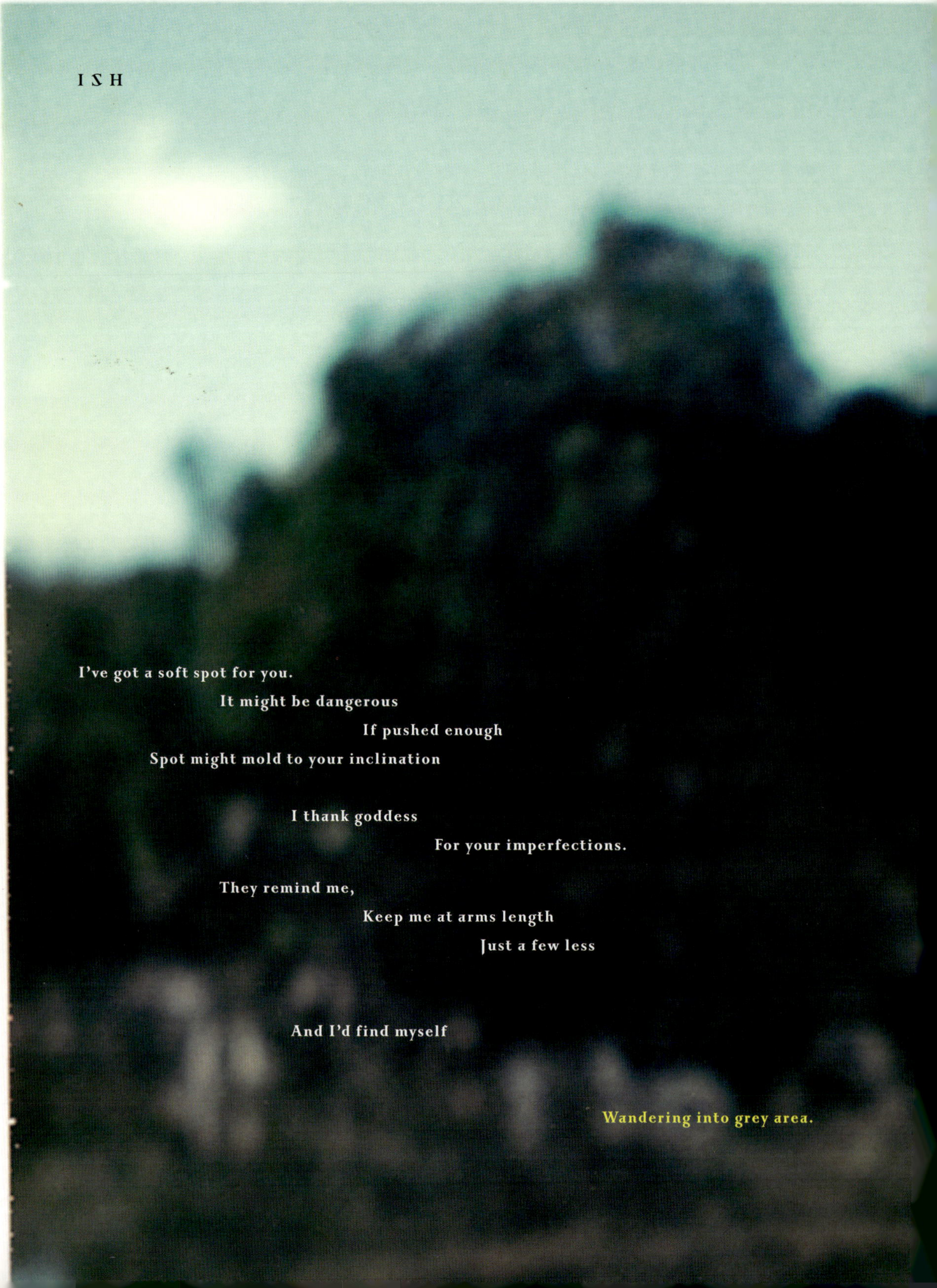

I've got a soft spot for you.
        It might be dangerous
                If pushed enough
      Spot might mold to your inclination

            I thank goddess
                    For your imperfections.

    They remind me,
             Keep me at arms length
                  Just a few less

        And I'd find myself

                          Wandering into grey area.

PSYCHOBABBLE

Such a lively and mercurial person you are. Constantly interupting the flow of circumstance as a conscious speed-bump towards that perverbial brick wall. Haven't we, after so many ~~illicited~~ mishaps, seen that the wall is a construct of our own over-caffinated minds? For serious, Yo. Aren't things getting just a wee- bit ridiculous around here?

I have never seen so many blatant signals pointing at the demise of civilization and so much ineptitude to do anything about it. Why don't we just call it a day and have a cosmic yard sale in hopes that perhaps we could sell off the better remaining parts of ourselves! At least then we could walk away with something to show for it.

At this rate, there will be nothing left but dust and non-biodegratibles. Which will indeed become the housing for some single celled organism 2 aeons later that eventually will have a brain large enough to become vain and marvel at the progress they have made around the time they figure out how to put a Starbucks at every street corner and make it seem like a good idea to everyone passing by. That inorganic housing left behind by the trogladytes would have been the perfect evolutionary cheat sheet for that first, single celled organism, giving it the perfect excuse to mutate just left of 'intended'.

What would have been your average, everyday humanoid cleaning the kitchen, (4,000,000 years later) into an average, everyday humanoid cleaning the kitchen but with the curious ability to microwave his/her hand without fear of harm! Advantage!

And it's advantages, seeming chaotic, circumstancial advantages that give us silly humans the advantage over other life forms. But darned the blasted conscience!

Constantly interupting the flow of cicumstance as a sub-conscious speed bump towards that perverbial brick wall. Why the flaw? Was the non-biodegratible left for us not 4,000,000 years earlier not 2 inches far enough to the left to catch the sun at that crucial time of day? Did a rival, single celled organism try and get nasty with you on some nuclear morning and knock the plastic whathaveyou off it's balance? Forever adulterating the growth of our hero!

For serious, Yo.

I'm backing the yard sale.

DOWN 101 IN OUR STEEL, FUCHSIA BOX...

ABOVE OUR HEADS EXISTS AN INFINITY OF UNFATHOMABLE FANTASIASTICS;

Below us, and the wheels of our steel box, resides the mammoth mole-hill of molecules; who, in fact, are bitter today after close scrutiny of their role in supporting ten billion sweaty feet for a mere two incarnations a day.

Behind us lies the things we just did and thought and were and would have, and everything else dressed in the fuzzy, shag beanie of "past-tense."

in front of us, giant green, street signs patiently contemplate over who will take their advice next. While the fates that we create rush at us like magnet to metal.

And within us lies the "blanket fresh outa the dryer" solace that reminds us why "the present" is called the "present."

AND FIELDS OF FUTURE FIRESIDE FABLES TRAIL CLOSE BEHIND.

"Tell all the truth...
but tell it slant,
Truth must dazzle gradually,
else every man be blind."

— Emily Dickinson

"Decreased rigidity,
increased creativity,
less compulsion,
more sense
of choice."

— R.A.W.

FIGURE ONE

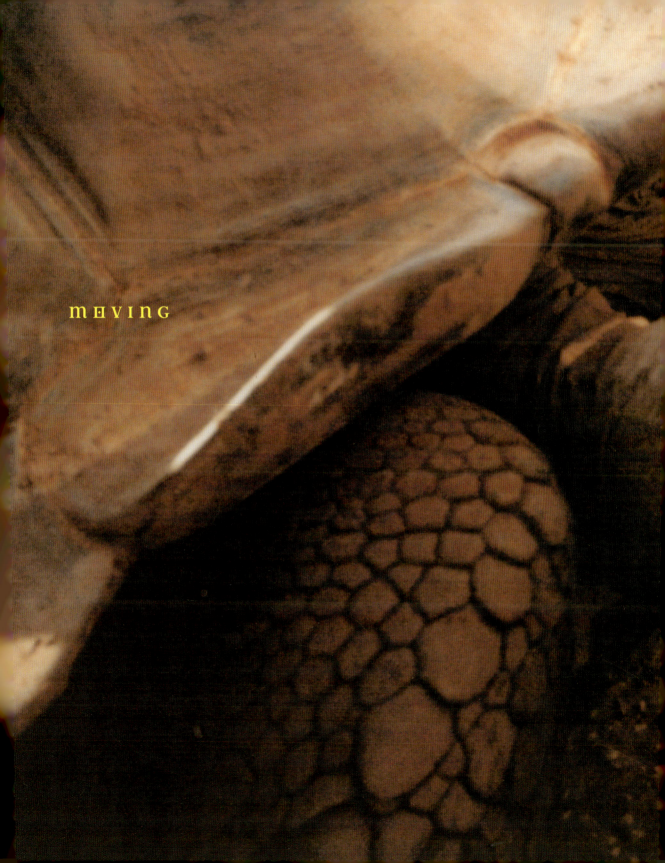

★ Little Kitten, Big Litter Box

    Nebulaes bloom, planets collide, and comets zoom around the checkerboard like a bratty, little brother on his new, blue bike leaving snail trails of ice in his wake.

    Ancient cosmic afterbirth floats helplessly on it's own inertia waiting impatiently for the next bullying gas giant to nudge it towards it's next ~~helpless~~ destination and I sit in a Thai Restaraunt bashing in the curry, fretting over the uncertainty of the dawn.

    I need to arm myself like a rodent lower on the food chain readying itself for the next attack from all sides.

    The voice inside the box is certain that if I get what he has my armor will be complete, my hole will be filled, and the bombardment will cease.

    "This sweater does this, that gadget does those, and this magazine will address the most →

pertinent aspects of my... dot, dot, dot, com" and I believe him! I don't want to but I do.

I am a little kitten in a big, shit filled litter box and I share this facility with a billion other fiercely independant felines who want badly to arm themselves too against the burdens of uncertainty and keep their paws clean in the meantime! meantime, meantime, meantime...

Yet the more I dig, the more I consume the more I unfold, the less protected I feel.

I am the spit on the hair of a son of an electron swimming around the nucleus of a cell inside the sperm of a killer bee and my purpose is as nebulous as why we've been bestowed with the capacity to give a shit

Music:
They just don't write songs like they used to, do they? The 1950's through the 1970's seemed a golden era of songwriting and it occured to me a few years ago that one of two things was happening; either bands, artists and songwriters of today aren't compsing the same caliber songs as we once experienced, or i am getting old. Firstly, I am definately not getting any younger and this I am ok with. Quite proud actually. But secondly, what ever happened to the ability to move the masses? Part thr seas with a simple word, melody and movement.(?)

We have the occasional burst of enlightened art which the world welcomes with open arms but because of it's scarce presence, we glutton ourselves on said piece of art and within weeks of it's introduction to the community we are sick and tired of hearing that same fucking song on the radio for the 4000th time and would sooner choke on sand than subject our ears to it's ubiquity any longer! It's sad really. Almost makes people with a hint in their mind that they might have a special song on their hands go run and hide that thing as to not be the product of an artist's lynching in the near future.

It used to be that a song could change your life! make you remember who you were and resurface the feelings you felt whilst hearing it for the first time. It could inspire you to start a religion, protest a war, paint a picture, or better yet, start your own band.

It is quite ironic right now how I am feeling while composing these trivial words. I feel like the old dude defending the days of yor, preaching to the ones present the shortcomings of the youth and it's contributions of today. But I know I am not the only one who thinks this way. We are a unique generation in the sense that nothing that's been produced artistically in our lifetime was ever brand new. The newest and most exciting developments were mere throwbacks and or plagarisms of times long past but deeply missed.

Not totally a bad thing, but disheartening in the sense that it seems as if everything has been done. Peering into piano keys and or the frets of a guitar neck once offered a variable creative infinity! A playground for the willing and gifted to express and discover and destroy and rebuild! Now in the year 2003, we have reissues of reissues, tributes of tributes. And the children of once rock Gods circumsizing their parents obelisk creations.

I won't fully believe that everything has been done. Music is no different than words in the sense that it is the same elements just rearranged in new and creative ways. If everything had been done already than there would be no new stories. No new recipies, paintings or inventions! And there are. Everyday something new is born into the world. Different than what came before and more prepared to withstand the elements. The problem with music is that we are putting our attention onto and into the wrong places. And overlooking the genuine articles because of our learned behaviors. The quick fix mentality has hindered our sight and we need to adjust our lenses to the less obvious once again. But is it too late?

German essentials

"fotzenlappen" - pussylips
"Hallo" - Hello
"Vee-gets-oysh" - how is everybody?
"Vier-vill-den-Soundman-thicken?"
        who wants to sleep with the
                Soundman?

"eea-zite-gyle!" - you guys are great!

"eesh-leeba-oysh" - I love you! (everyone)
     (deesh) one person.

"feela-dank-das-ia-das-ide"
     - thankyou for coming!

"du haus chuna owgen." - you have beaut
                                eyes.

"danka" - thankyou.

I HAD THAT DREAM AGAIN...
I'M EXPLORING MY (OWN) HOME,
I HAPPEN ACROSS A DOOR,
THAT LEADS ME TO A ROOM I'VE NEVER

LIKE SALT TO THE OCEAN,
SO ARE METAPHORS TO THE MIND.

stir content sift through